T0198958

My Two Houses

Terrance Davis
Illustrated by Joe Lee

AuthorHouse™
1663 Liberty Drive
Bloomington, IN 47403
www.authorhouse.com
Phone: 1-800-839-8640

First published by AuthorHouse   7/26/2011

ISBN: 978-1-4634-1301-9 (sc)

Library of Congress Control Number: 2011909327

Printed in the United States of America

Certain stock imagery © Thinkstock.

This book is printed on acid-free paper.

authorHOUSE®

My two houses I love them both.
But which one do I love the most?

At mommy's house I am the king.
She lets me do almost anything.

At daddy's house I'm just an heir that stands beside his great big chair.

In the morning mommy wakes me up so we can go and eat.

She makes me anything I want and that is just a treat!

But daddy, I try to wake him up because he sleeps too long.

I try to push him out of bed but he is just too strong.

At mommy's house I have lots of toys.
I play with them all day.

But daddy says it's too much noise and he puts them all away.

I try to stay really quiet until daddy says he's through.

And when he comes to play with me it's amazing what he can do!

He can toss me and he can throw me.
He can help me fly around.

And when he reads me stories, he can make each and every sound.

Daddy can throw and daddy can catch.
Daddy can run until I fall.

Mommy can catch and mommy can throw but
mommy doesn't run much at all.

At mommy's house I stay up late to, dance, play, and sing!

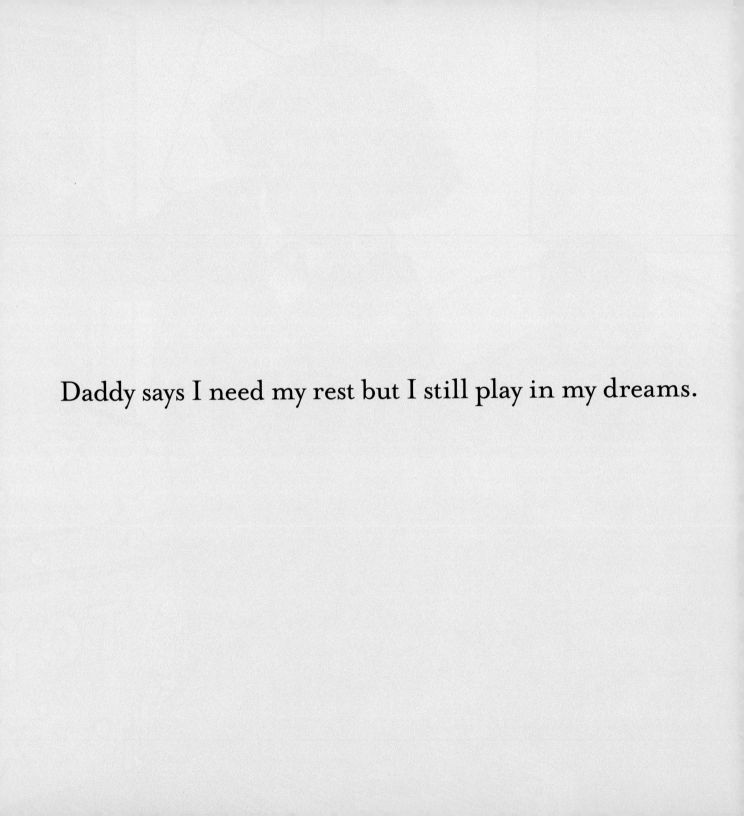

Daddy says I need my rest but I still play in my dreams.

My two houses I love them both.
I don't know which one I love the most.
I love them just the same!

Printed in the United States
By Bookmasters